Explore!

ANCIENT GREEKS

Jane Bingham

Published in 2015 by Wayland

Copyright © Wayland 2015

Wayland
338 Euston Road
London NW1 3BH

Wayland Australia
Level 17/207 Kent Street
Sydney, NSW 2000

Produced for Wayland by
White-Thomson Publishing
www.wtpub.co.uk
+44 (0)843 208 7460

Editor: Jane Bingham
Designer: Elaine Wilkinson
Picture researcher: Jane Bingham
Illustrations for step-by-step: Stefan Chabluk
Map illustration: Wayland
Proof reader: Lucy Ross

A cataloguing record for this title is available
from the British Library.

ISBN 978 0 7502 889 89
eBook ISBN 978 0 7502 8531 5
Dewey Number 938-dc23

First published in 2014 by Wayland

Printed in China

Wayland is a division of Hachette Children's
Books, an Hachette UK company

www.hachette.co.uk

Picture acknowledgements:
The author and publisher would like to thank the
following agencies and people for allowing these
pictures to be reproduced:
Cover (top left) Dimitrios/Shutterstock; (top right) Fedor
Korolevskiy/Shutterstock; (bottom left) meirion matthias/
Shutterstock; (bottom right) Mikadun/Shutterstock;
p.1(left) Alexandre Fagundes De Fagundes/Dreamstime;
(right) Wikimedia; p.3 (left) Panos Karas/Shutterstock;
(right) Ariy/Shutterstock;p.5 (top) Dan Breckwoldt/
Dreamstime; (bottom) Christos Georghiou/ Shutterstock;
p.6 Photoscreation/Shutterstock; p.7 (top) Marina
Samokhina/Dreamstime; (bottom) Wikimedia; p.8 Panos
Karas/Shutterstock; p.9 (top) S. Borisov/ Shutterstock;
(middle) abxyz/Shutterstock; (bottom) Wikimedia; p.10
Wikimedia; p.11 (top) Fedor Korolevskiy/Shutterstock;
(bottom) Styve Reineck/ Shutterstock; p.12 Wikimedia;
p.13 (top) Payne, Roger (b.1934)/Private Collection/
Look and Learn/The Bridgeman Art Library; (bottom)
Wikimedia; p.14 Wikimedia; p.15 (top) Alexandre
Fagundes De Fagundes/Dreamstime; (bottom) Wikimedia;
p.16 Wikimedia; p.17 (top) Sophy Kozlova/Dreamstime;
(bottom) Mircea Nicolescu/Dreamstime; p.18 Gaertner
Heinrich (1828-1909) (after)/Private Collection/
Archives Charmet/The Bridgeman Art Library; p.19
(top) Wikimedia; (bottom) andersphoto/Shutterstock;
p.20 (left) Panos Karas/Shutterstock; (middle) Ariy/
Shutterstock; (right) Wikimedia; p.22 Lefteris Papaulakis/
Dreamstime; p.23 (top) Morphart Creation/Shutterstock;
(bottom) offscreen/Dreamstime; p.24 Zack Frank/
Shutterstock; p.25 (top) Joraba/Dreamstime; (bottom)
Dimitrios/Shutterstock; p.26 Louvre,Paris,France/
Giraudon/The Bridgeman Art Library; p.27 (top)
Kmiragaya/Dreamstime; (bottom) Anastasios71/
Shutterstock; p.28 (top) Wikimedia; (bottom) John
Copland/Shutterstock; p.29 (top) Calvindexter/
Dreamstime; (bottom left) Wikimedia; (bottom right)
andersphoto/Shutterstock; p.31 abxyz/Shutterstock;
p.32 Panos Karas/Shutterstock.

Contents

Who were the ancient Greeks?

Around 2,500 years ago, the people of ancient Greece created a way of life that has been copied and admired ever since. Ancient Greece has been called the birthplace of western civilization.

The Greek world

The ancient Greeks lived on the mainland and islands of Greece and along a strip of the Turkish coast. But their influence reached far beyond their homelands. They traded throughout the Mediterranean region, and Alexander the Great conquered an empire that included Egypt and large parts of Asia.

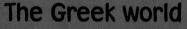

MACEDONIA

GREECE

TURKEY

Delphi

Argos Corinth

Olympia Mycenae Athens

Sparta

Mediterranean Sea

Crete

This map shows the main cities of ancient Greece in around 600BCE. In 338BCE the kingdom of Macedonia became part of Greece.

The Parthenon in Athens was dedicated to Athena, the city's patron goddess.

Amazing Athens

Athens was the leading city in Greece. It was home to some outstanding writers, artists and thinkers. The Athenians also developed a method of government known as democracy. Instead of being ruled by a king, they voted for a group of leaders to run their state.

A lasting influence

Today, we still design buildings in the classical style developed by the Greeks. Countries around the world are run as democracies, and mathematicians and scientists use Greek ideas and theories. Greek myths and legends are still retold, Greek plays are performed, and athletes compete in the Olympic Games, which began in ancient Greece.

The ancient Greeks told very exciting stories. This picture by a modern artist shows the hero Hercules fighting a giant lion.

Early Greeks

The first great civilization in ancient Greece developed on the island of Crete around 2000BCE. The Minoans lived in small, well-organized communities, ruled by powerful kings. Their most famous ruler was King Minos of Knossos.

Minoans

Minoan civilization was organized around its cities. Each city had a palace which was surrounded by many smaller houses. The Minoans were skilled painters and potters. They had a simple form of writing, and traded across the Mediterranean Sea.

Minoan palaces were painted brilliant colours. This is part of the royal palace at Knossos on the island of Crete.

The Lion Gate at Mycenae has a pair of lionesses carved over it. It was once the grand entranceway to the city.

Mycenaeans

Around 1600BCE, a new civilization emerged on mainland Greece. The Mycenaeans were ruled by kings who lived in palaces inside walled cities. One of their largest cities was Mycenae, and the remains of its palace can still be seen today. The Mycenaeans believed in life after death, so they buried their kings with all the treasures they might need in the next world. Archaeologists have found cups, weapons and jewellery, as well as golden masks made to cover a king's face.

Wars and chaos

The Mycenaeans were fierce warriors who fought many battles to gain land. One of these struggles may have been the Trojan War, described by the Greek poet Homer in his famous poem *The Iliad*. After 1200BCE, the Mycenaeans began to face defeat in war, and their civilization slowly came to an end. The years between 1100 and 800BCE are sometimes called the Greek Dark Ages. In this period, people struggled to survive and the skills of metalwork, pottery and writing were lost.

A royal death mask from a Mycenaean tomb. When it was first discovered the mask was believed to show the face of Agamemnon, a hero of the Trojan War. But this theory was later proved to be wrong.

A great civilization

The Greek Dark Ages lasted until around 800BCE, when people began to make pots again. Gradually, the Greeks started trading and even rediscovered the skill of writing. On the mainland, city-states developed, with communities of people clustered around a city. Athens, Sparta, Corinth and Argos were all great city-states.

The Persian wars

The Greek city-states saw each other as rivals, but they still united to face foreign enemies. Their greatest threat came from the mighty Persian Empire. The Persians tried three times to invade the Greek lands, and each time the Greeks managed to drive them back.

This statue shows Leonidas, King of the Spartans. He led the Greek Army against the Persians at the Battle of Thermopylae in 480BCE.

Athens versus Sparta

After the Persian wars ended in 449BCE, Athens was rebuilt. Under their leader, Pericles, the Athenians developed a system of democratic government and Athens became a centre for art, architecture, philosophy and science. The Spartans, however, saw the growth of Athens as a threat. For almost 30 years Athens and Sparta fought the Peloponnesian Wars, which finally ended when Athens surrendered in 404BCE.

Pericles made Athens into a great democratic state. He was also responsible for the rebuilding of the Acropolis - a raised rocky platform where all the most important buildings stood.

The rise of Macedonia

By the 350s BCE, the city-states were weakening, However, another region was growing in strength. In 359BCE, King Philip II became the new ruler of the northern kingdom of Macedonia. He began to conquer the surrounding lands and in 338BCE he won control of Greece. Philip took command of the Greek Army and prepared to go to war with Persia, but he died before the campaign began. He was succeeded by his son, Alexander, who went on to build an enormous empire.

Alexander was an outstanding army general. His amazing victories earned him the title 'Alexander the Great'.

The Greek world

In the space of just twelve years, Alexander transformed the Greek world. He won an empire that included Egypt and Persia (modern-day Iran) and stretched as far east as India.

In 333BCE, Alexander's army won a great victory over the Persians at the Battle of Issus. This mosaic shows King Darius of Persia escaping from the battlefield.

Alexander's victories

Alexander's first move was to drive the Persians out of Turkey. Then he went on to conquer Egypt. In 331BCE, he gained control of the vast Persian Empire, and started to march into India. By this time, however, his troops were very tired. Alexander agreed to return to Persia where he caught a fever and died, at the age of 32.

Coins with the head of Alexander were used all over his empire.

Alexander's empire

Even though he died young, Alexander still left his mark on his empire. He founded 70 cities, including the port of Alexandria in Egypt. Alexander's empire was not ruled from Greece. Apart from appointing a few Greek governors, he relied on local rulers to control his lands. He also respected local traditions and customs. After being crowned King of Persia, he wore Persian dress and married a Persian woman called Roxanne.

This temple at Kom Ombo in Egypt was built by a Greek ruler. It combines Greek and Egyptian architectural styles.

After Alexander

After Alexander's death, the Greeks gradually lost control of Persia, although they continued to rule in Egypt. A Greek family called the Ptolemies ruled Egypt for 300 years, but in 30BCE they were defeated by the Romans. Egypt was the last of the Greek lands to be conquered. By the time it fell, the Romans were very powerful and the Greek age had come to an end.

Everyday life

Houses in ancient Greece were usually made from mud. Poor families lived in simple shelters, while wealthy people had large, comfortable homes built around a courtyard. Their houses had a dining room for entertaining guests and an upper floor for the family rooms.

Greek men and women wore loose-fitting robes made from wool or linen. Older men usually wore long robes. Young men and boys dressed in short tunics.

Men

Most Greek men worked as farmers, fishermen or craftworkers. Some joined the army and others became merchants, travelling by ship all over the Mediterranean region. Educated men trained to be lawyers, priests and politicians.

Women

Women spent most of their time at home, running the household. Rich women had many slaves to supervise and only very poor families had no household slaves. Women of all classes made the family's clothes, spinning thread and weaving cloth on a loom.

Children

Girls in ancient Greece did not go to school. Instead, they stayed at home and learned how to be good wives and mothers. Most boys helped their fathers with their work, but a few went to school. Their education began at the age of seven and had three stages. At the first school, pupils learned reading, writing and arithmetic. At the second, they studied poetry and music, and at the third, they were taught dancing and athletics.

This picture shows a teacher with his pupil. The boy is learning to write on a wax tablet.

Slaves

It has been estimated that around half the population of ancient Greece were slaves. Many were prisoners-of-war, while others were the children of slaves or had been sold into slavery because their parents could not afford to raise them. Most slaves worked in homes, on farms or in workshops, but some had very hard lives labouring in mines and quarries.

This carving shows a wealthy woman with her household slave. The slave is caring for the baby of her mistress.

Gods and goddesses

People in ancient Greece worshipped many gods and goddesses. Zeus was the chief god and ruler of the skies. Hera, his wife, was the goddess of women and marriage. Apollo was the sun god and Aphrodite was the goddess of love and beauty.

Honouring the gods

The Greeks built large stone temples for their gods. Inside each temple was a statue of the god, which only the priests could visit. On certain days of the year, priests held public ceremonies. They stood on the temple porch and sacrificed animals to please the gods.

Nike was the goddess of victory. She was often shown running very fast.

The remains of the temple at Delphi, where the oracle lived.

Oracles and omens

When people had important decisions to make, they asked the gods for advice. They believed the gods could speak through special priests and priestesses, known as oracles. The most famous oracle lived in the temple of Apollo at Delphi. People travelled from all over the Greek world to ask her for guidance. Priests also looked for signs (or omens) of the will of the gods. After they had sacrificed an animal, they examined its organs (such as the heart or lungs) and interpreted the patterns made by them. Then the priests explained the meaning of these omens.

Stories of the gods

People told many stories about their gods. In one story, a princess called Arachne challenged the goddess Athene to a weaving contest. When Athene realized how well Arachne could weave, she was furious and turned her into a spider. The Greeks used this story to explain why spiders weave such wonderful webs.

Athene was the goddess of wisdom, war and weaving. She was also the patron of Athens.

Games and plays

In their leisure time, the Greeks enjoyed going to the theatre and watching sporting contests. These events were often part of a religious festival that could include dancing, singing, plays and athletics.

Boxing was a popular Olympic sport. Contestants protected their hands and wrists with strips of leather.

The Olympic Games

Festivals with athletics contests were held in many parts of Greece, but the biggest sporting event of all was the Olympic Games, which took place in Olympia. The Olympics were held every four years as part of a festival for Zeus. They lasted for five days and included running, chariot racing, wrestling and boxing. At the end of the Games, each winner was presented with a wreath of laurel leaves.

Plays were performed in enormous open-air theatres. Actors needed to be easily seen, so they wore masks and wigs, padded clothes and thick-soled shoes.

Early plays

Plays were first performed as part of a festival to Dionysius, the god of pleasure. They were spoken by a group of men, called a chorus, and included lots of dancing and singing. Later, actors played individual parts and gradually their scenes became the most important part of the plays.

Tragedies and comedies

Greek plays soon developed into two types. Tragedies were usually about heroes from Greek myths. They explored serious subjects, such as ambition or envy, and they usually had a sad ending. Comedies were about ordinary people. They contained jokes about Greek society and ended happily. The tragedies of Aeschylus, Sophocles and Euripides, and the comedies of Aristophanes are still performed today.

This is a modern performance of *Oedipus Rex*, a tragedy by Sophocles.

17

A day at the Olympic Games

This fictional letter describes the experience of a spectator at the Olympic Games around 350BCE. It is written by a young athlete to his friend.

Dear Dorian,

I've just had the most exciting week of my life! We arrived in Olympia the day before the Games began, so there was plenty of time to look around. There are three running tracks, an arena for wrestling

and boxing, and a hippodrome for the horse-racing events. But the most amazing sight of all is the statue of Zeus — made of gold and ivory and ten times bigger than father!

The first day was taken up with the opening ceremony, and then the Games began. There were boys' running races, followed by the pankration and wrestling. The pankration got very rough, with fighters rolling around in the mud, and several fingers were broken!

The third day was my favourite. After a sacrifice of 100 oxen to Zeus, we watched the chariot races. Then came the pentathlon – sprinting, long jump, discus, javelin and wrestling all in one incredible contest!

The last sporting event was the hoplitodromia – a 200-metre sprint by athletes wearing helmets and armour and carrying shields. Just imagine running with all that weight!

On the final day, the winners were presented with their laurel wreaths and everyone joined in an enormous feast.

The moment I get home, I'm going to start training. I need to be really fit to be selected for the next Games in four years' time!

Your friend,

Alexis

The letter on these pages has been imagined for this book. Can you create your own letter from a child living in ancient Greece? Use the facts in this book and in other sources to help you write your letter.

Make an actor's mask

Actors in ancient Greece wore masks to show different characters and feelings. We know what these masks looked like because images of them have survived in pottery and sculpture. The masks on this page show a wise old man, a sweet young woman and a wicked mischief-maker. Why not make your own actor's mask and act out a play with your friends?

You will need:
bendy card
pencil
scissors
crayons or felt-tip pens
cotton wool
coloured wool
glue stick
elastic

1 Place a small plate on your piece of card and draw around it. Then draw a face in the middle of your circle. Make the mouth and eye-holes very large.

2 Cut out the circle shape. Then carefully cut out holes for the mouth and eyes. Colour in the mask and stick on some cotton wool or coloured wool for hair.

3 Make two small holes close to the outer edges of the mask. Thread a strip of elastic through the holes and knot it at both ends. Now you have a mask you can wear over your face.

4 Work out a short play to act with your friends. It could be based on a Greek myth. As well as wearing your mask, you can wrap a sheet around your body so you look like an ancient Greek actor!

Medicine, science and maths

Greek scholars studied the world around them and tried to understand how it worked. Their ideas and discoveries provided the foundations for the later study of medicine, science and maths.

Medicine

The first Greek doctors were priests of Asclepius, the god of healing. They believed that diseases were a punishment from the gods and they tried to heal people with charms and prayers. However, around 400BCE, a scholar called Hippocrates introduced a new approach to medicine. He studied the human body and tried to work out the causes of diseases. Then he prescribed herbal medicines, special diets and rest or exercise. The followers of Hippocrates founded medical schools to teach his ideas and Greek doctors became famous throughout the ancient world.

A statue of Asclepius, the god of medicine. He holds a staff with a snake coiled around it.

Archimedes invented the Archimedes screw, a machine for lifting water. This diagram has been cut away to show how it worked.

Science

Archimedes is the most famous of all the Greek scientists. He was an outstanding mathematician, astronomer, engineer and inventor. He discovered an important scientific rule when he noticed that the water in his bathtub overflowed as he stepped into it. From this observation, he worked out that an object always displaces its own volume of water.

Maths

Euclid worked in Alexandria around the year 300BCE. He discovered many rules about geometrical shapes and is often called the 'father of geometry'. Euclid's ideas were developed by Pythagoras, who lived a century later. He created a famous theorem (rule) for calculating the size of angles in triangles. His ideas are still used in maths today.

Pythagoras lived on the island of Samos and had a large group of followers.

Architects and builders

Greek architects aimed to create buildings that looked simple, elegant and balanced. Their designs have been copied throughout the world.

This copy of the Parthenon in Nashville, Tennessee, USA, gives some idea how it would have looked when it was first built. However, the original would have been much more colourful!

Temple designs

Greek temples were constructed from a few basic elements: a set of vertical columns, known as capitals; four horizontal beams resting on the capitals; and a sloping roof. Capitals were built in two main styles. Doric capitals were left very plain, while Ionic capitals had a scroll-like pattern carved at the top. Architects followed strict mathematical rules to make sure the balance of the different elements was pleasing to the eye.

Building a temple

Temples were built from heavy blocks of marble or limestone that were cut and carved by expert masons. Builders stood on a wooden scaffolding and the blocks were winched up to them using a pulley and ropes. There was no cement to hold the blocks together. Instead, a metal rod ran through the centre of all the blocks, and held them firmly in place.

These Ionic capitals were constructed from carved blocks of stone placed one above the other.

Carving and decoration

Most Greek temples were decorated with carved and painted figures. A series of scenes formed a horizontal frieze that ran across the front of the building and sometimes continued along the sides as well. The triangular space above the frieze was called the pediment. It was filled with larger-than-life carved figures. A few buildings had carved female figures instead of columns. These giant supporting statues are called caryatids.

Caryatids support the porch of the Erechtheum, a temple on the Acropolis.

Artists, writers and thinkers

The ancient Greeks are famous for their beautiful sculptures, vases and metalwork. Writers produced poems and histories, and philosophers considered the meaning of life.

Sculpture

Ancient Greek sculpture can be divided into three main styles. Carvings from the Archaic period (around 488–480BCE) were influenced by Egyptian art and look stiff and formal. Sculptors in the Classical age (around 480–323BCE) showed the human body in a more natural way, carving calm and beautiful figures. Figures from the Hellenistic period (around 323–100BCE) are dramatic and full of movement, and express powerful emotions.

A Roman copy of the head of Aphrodite by the Greek sculptor, Praxiteles. He was the outstanding master of the Greek classical style and his work was often copied by other sculptors.

Pottery

Potters made vases in a range of shapes and sizes, and decorated them with patterns, figures and scenes. The finest pottery was made in Athens between around 550 and 300BCE. Early vases had black figures on a red background. Vases made after 530BCE generally had red figures against a black background.

A painted vase showing a chariot rider. Vases were often decorated with scenes of daily life or figures from Greek myths.

Writers and philosophers

The Greeks wrote short love poems and long epic poems telling stories. The famous poet Homer composed two epic poems: *The Iliad*, which tells the story of the Trojan War; and *The Odyssey*, which describes a difficult journey made by the warrior Odysseus. The writer Herodotus was the first known author to gather historical facts and put them together in an exciting narrative. The leading Greek philosophers were Socrates and his pupil Plato. They explored ideas about the way the world works and how people should behave.

Socrates taught his students by asking them difficult questions. Philosophers have followed this teaching method ever since.

Facts and figures

The ancient Greeks invented the yo-yo. Greek yo-yos were made from wood, metal or terracotta.

The bull was a sacred animal in Minoan culture. Sculptors carved statues of bulls and young men and women practised the dangerous custom of leaping over a bull's back!

After the Greek victory at the Battle of Marathon, a runner was sent to Athens, which was 26 miles (42 kilometres) away. As soon as he had announced the good news, he dropped down dead. Modern marathon races are named after this famous run.

Children from the city-state of Sparta were sent to military training school at the age of seven. Boys and girls went to different schools but they were all taught to fight and wrestle.

The ancient Greeks played an important part in the development of the alphabet. The first two letters of the Greek alphabet – alpha and beta – have given us the word 'alphabet'.

During the Olympic Games, all wars stopped. There was a truce for a month so athletes from all over the Greek world could compete in the Games.

Athletes who cheated in the Games had to pay heavy fines, and one athlete who backed out of a contest was fined for cowardice!

There were no gold, silver or bronze awards in the ancient Olympics, just a laurel wreath for the winner of each event.

Glossary

astronomer Someone who studies the stars, sun and moon and other planets.

BCE The letters BCE stand for 'before common era'. They refer to dates before the birth of Christ.

campaign A series of actions intended to achieve a goal.

capital A column, usually carved from stone.

CE The letters CE stand for 'common era'. They refer to dates after the birth of Christ.

city-state A city and its surrounding lands that is independent and is governed by leaders in the city.

civilization A well-organized society.

classical Made by the Romans or ancient Greeks, or copying the Romans or Greeks.

community A group of people living in the same place and sharing the same customs.

democracy A system of government in which leaders are voted for by the people.

displace Take the place of something.

epic A long poem telling the story of a hero.

fictional Made up or invented.

frieze A horizontal band of decoration.

mainland A large area of land that forms the main part of a country.

narrative A series of connected events that tell a story.

observation A statement based on something that has been seen or noticed.

oracle A priest or priestess in ancient Greece who was believed to have powers to predict the future.

pankration A sporting contest held at the ancient Olympic Games in which opponents fought each other by boxing, wrestling and kicking.

patron A person or a god who gives their support to a group of people or a city.

philosopher Someone who asks questions about how the world works and comes up with ideas and theories.

prescribe To give medicine or instructions to a patient.

scholar Someone who studies a subject in depth.

spectator Someone who watches a show, sport or other event.

surrender To stop resisting an enemy.

traditions Customs that have been handed down through many generations

volume The amount of space that an object takes up.

Further reading

Ancient Greece (Find Out About), Colin Hynson (Wayland, 2008)

Ancient Greeks (Hail!), Jen Green (Wayland, 2013)

Ancient Greeks (Craft Box), Jillian Powell (Wayland, 2013)

Ancient Greece (Food and Cooking In), Clive Gifford (Wayland, 2009)

Greek Soldiers (Greatest Warriors), Alex Stewart (Franklin Watts, 2013)

Websites

http://www.ancientgreece.co.uk/
A beautifully illustrated site by The British Museum. It includes sections on daily life, festivals and games, gods and goddesses, and knowledge and learning. The sections include objects to explore and challenges to try.

http://www.bbc.co.uk/schools/primaryhistory/ancient_greeks/
A BBC website for children, with features on many aspects of life in ancient Greece including the home, Athens, Sparta and the Olympic Games. You can also play an interactive game, Greek Hero, that takes you on an adventure through ancient Greece.

http://www.pbs.org/empires/thegreeks/htmlver/
A PBS website on ancient Greece. It includes a feature on the making of the Acropolis with a 3D animation of the Parthenon and a video tour of the temple as it would once have looked.

http://www.olympic.org/ancient-olympic-games
A site devoted to the ancient Olympic Games. It has sections on the origins of the Games, famous athletes, and different sports. There is also a cartoon-style view of the Games.

Index